FORENSIC INVESTIGATIONS
OF THE
ANCIENT EGYPTIANS

James Bow

CRABTREE
PUBLISHING COMPANY
WWW.CRABTREEBOOKS.COM

Author: James Bow

Editors: Sarah Eason, John Andrews, Petrice Custance, and Janine Deschenes

Proofreader and indexer: Wendy Scavuzzo

Editorial director: Kathy Middleton

Design: Paul Myerscough, Paul Oakley, and Jane McKenna

Cover design: Paul Myerscough

Photo research: Rachel Blount

Production coordinator and Prepress technician: Tammy McGarr

Print coordinator: Katherine Berti

Consultant: John Malam

Produced for Crabtree Publishing Company by Calcium Creative Ltd.

Library and Archives Canada Cataloguing in Publication

Bow, James, 1972-, author
  Forensic investigations of the ancient Egyptians / James Bow.

(Forensic footprints of ancient worlds)
Includes index.
Issued in print and electronic formats.
ISBN 978-0-7787-4941-7 (hardcover).--
ISBN 978-0-7787-4954-7 (softcover).--
ISBN 978-1-4271-2114-1 (HTML)

  1. Egypt--Antiquities--Juvenile literature. 2. Forensic archaeology--Egypt--Juvenile literature. 3. Archaeology and history--Egypt--Juvenile literature. I. Title.

DT56.9.B68 2018   j932.00909   C2018-902977-3
                                              C2018-902978-1

Library of Congress Cataloging-in-Publication Data

Names: Bow, James, author.
Title: Forensic investigations of the ancient Egyptians / James Bow.
Description: New York : Crabtree Publishing, 2018. |
  Series: Forensic footprints of ancient worlds | Includes index.
Identifiers: LCCN 2018027910 (print) | LCCN 2018029211 (ebook) |
  ISBN 9781427121141 (Electronic) |
  ISBN 9780778749417 (hardcover) |
  ISBN 9780778749547 (pbk.)
Subjects: LCSH: Forensic archaeology--Egypt--Juvenile literature.
  | Egypt--Antiquities--Juvenile literature. | Mummies--Egypt--Juvenile literature.
Classification: LCC CC79.F67 (ebook) |
  LCC CC79.F67 B69 2018 (print) | DDC 932--dc23
LC record available at https://lccn.loc.gov/2018027910

Crabtree Publishing Company

www.crabtreebooks.com   1-800-387-7650

Printed in the U.S.A./092018/CG20180719

Published in Canada
Crabtree Publishing
616 Welland Ave.
St. Catharines, Ontario
L2M 5V6

Published in the United States
Crabtree Publishing
PMB 59051
350 Fifth Avenue, 59th Floor
New York, New York 10118

Published in the United Kingdom
Crabtree Publishing
Maritime House
Basin Road North, Hove
BN41 1WR

Published in Australia
Crabtree Publishing
3 Charles Street
Coburg North
VIC, 3058

CONTENTS

INVESTIGATING THE ANCIENT EGYPTIANS

One of the greatest **civilizations** ever known, ancient Egypt, began around 5,000 years ago. The ancient Egyptians lived along the Nile River in North Africa. They built the amazing pyramids, which were tombs for their **pharaohs**, or kings. The ancient Egyptians have fascinated people for centuries, and scientists and **archaeologists** are still trying to solve many mysteries about them.

Solving Mysteries

Scientists have learned a lot about the ancient Egyptians from **evidence** they left behind, such as their **hieroglyphs**, an ancient form of picture writing, and the tombs where they buried the dead. But there are still many mysteries to investigate, such as the secrets of the Great Pyramid of Giza and the **identity** of **mummified** bodies. Is there a way to solve these ancient mysteries? Yes—with **forensic science**!

DID
You Know?

Scientists at the University of Zurich, in Switzerland, studied more than 3,000 ancient Egyptian mummies and found that many of them had **decayed** teeth. Around 18 percent had rotten teeth, including **abscesses** and **cavities**. Tests show that the ancient Egyptians may have had such bad teeth because they ate a lot of sugary honey.

Mummified bodies are carefully unwrapped before forensic tests are carried out on teeth or bones.

Ancient Egyptian paintings tell us much about how the ancient Egyptians lived. This painting tells us about how they saw their pharaohs. Here, a pharaoh greets Thoth, a god with the head of a bird. This tells us that the ancient Egyptians believed their pharaohs were so important that they could talk to the gods.

X-rays of ancient teeth can tell forensic experts if the person had a bad or healthy diet.

HOW SCIENCE SOLVED THE PAST:
FORENSIC FOOTPRINTS

To solve crimes, forensic scientists examine evidence from the places where crimes took place, called **crime scenes**. The **techniques** that they use to solve crimes are also used by people to solve mysteries about the past. Archaeologists and **anthropologists** study the clues, or forensic footprints, ancient people left behind to find out more about them. Archaeologists use forensic techniques to find out about ancient buildings and **sites**. Anthropologists use forensic techniques to learn more about ancient peoples from their skeletons and the objects they left behind.

SOLVING PAST MYSTERIES

Forensic scientists can help police find a body in a recent crime scene and they can also find out where bodies were buried long ago. They dig up any items buried with the bodies, carefully make a note of them, and **preserve** them. They then use forensic science to find out more about the bodies and items.

Raiding the Remains

Just as forensic scientists study skeletons or bodies to solve mysteries about a crime, they study ancient **remains** to find out who people were. They can carry out tests to find out when and why they died. Using the skulls of the dead, scientists can also use special **scanners** and computers to model their faces.

So, what clues, or forensic footprints, did the ancient Egyptians leave behind and what can we learn from them? Let's follow their forensic footprint trail!

At ancient sites, forensic scientists make notes and drawings of what they find, as well as where they find it. Then they carry out tests using the latest technology to figure out information, such as the age of the stones seen above, found at the city of Luxor, Egypt.

Forensic experts rebuilt the face of this ancient Egyptian woman. She was 50–60 years old when she died.

HOW SCIENCE SOLVED THE PAST:

MODELING MYSTERIES

We cannot visit the past, but we can model it. Forensic scientists use clues from ancient sites to figure out how the buildings that once stood there looked. For example, **foundations** in the ground hint at where walls might have been. Areas in which broken pottery is buried hint at garbage sites. Using this information, archaeologists use a computer to create a **three-dimensional (3-D)** model of the site as it might once have been. This helps them learn about how the buildings were made and what they might have been used for.

Forensic scientists can also use clues from the past to make 3-D models of people who lived long ago. They study skulls and skeletons to figure out what a person looked like. They then use that information to create a 3-D model of the person.

DID You Know?

Today, forensic scientists are using the latest technology to bring ancient Egypt back to life! Using evidence from ancient sites, forensic scientists are helping archaeologists build 3-D models of ancient Egypt. They have created a **virtual reality (VR)** world. Wearing special goggles, you can explore this virtual ancient Egypt! You can enter the pharaoh's burial site, examine the magnificent tombs, climb inside the **Sphinx**, and climb onboard an impressive wooden trading boat that is 4,600 years old.

MUMMY FORENSICS

The ancient Egyptians left many forensic clues for us to find. Some of the most exciting clues they left behind are their mummies. These are the preserved bodies of the dead.

Inside a Mummy

Forensic scientists use a lot of different tools to investigate crimes, and they use the same tools to examine mummies. X-ray machines allow forensic scientists to examine the inside of a mummy and see its bones. Tiny cameras on the end of a small wire can be slipped inside a mummy to send photos back to the scientists. **Magnetic resonance imaging (MRI)** machines, which examine people in the hospital, can also build a 3-D computer image of the insides of a mummy.

Mummies were covered in hundreds of yards of wrappings. It could take as long as two weeks to wrap a mummy from head to toe!

Mummy Study

By studying a mummy, we can learn the age of that person and whether they were male or female. Scientists can discover what the person ate, and if he or she had a disease such as cancer or heart disease. They can even figure out if the person was related to another mummy!

So much can be discovered from the forensic study of ancient Egyptian mummies that the field has its own name: Mummy Forensics!

X-rays allow scientists to examine a mummy without needing to take off its wrappings. This ensures that the mummy is not damaged.

DIGGING DEEP WITH DNA

DNA stands for deoxyribonucleic acid. It is a special **molecule** that is found in the **cells** of most living things. What a living thing looks like and how it grows is ruled by DNA. Scientists use DNA tests to discover many facts about anything that was once alive.

Pass It On

DNA is passed to a child from its father and mother. This is why scientists look for DNA evidence to identify bodies and link people to families. **Biomolecular archaeology** is the study of ancient DNA from remains such as bones and teeth. By comparing the DNA from different bodies, scientists can find out where different groups of people lived. They can also tell who they may have married. But DNA does not have to be human to be useful. Studying the DNA of plants or animals from ancient Egypt also tells us more about the world of the Egyptians.

*This DNA shape, which looks like a twisted ladder, is called a double helix. Under powerful **microscopes**, forensic scientists study all the different parts of the DNA molecule to find out as much as they can about the living thing it came from.*

DID You Know?

In 1985, scientists extracted the very first DNA evidence from an ancient human. Scientists tested 23 mummies of different ages, but it was the mummy of a one-year-old Egyptian boy that produced the DNA.

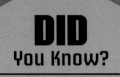

Tricky Testing

DNA studies can be tricky. Substances used to preserve ancient bodies can change or destroy DNA. However, scientists are getting better and better at DNA studies and at protecting bodies during tests without changing their DNA.

Scientists study a skull for signs of damage that might have been caused deliberately. This could mean the person was murdered or killed in battle. For example, a hole in the skull could have been caused by a blow from an object.

HOW SCIENCE SOLVED THE PAST:

THE MYSTERY OF THE TWO BROTHERS

The bodies of Khnum-Nakht and Nakht-Ankh were found together in a tomb **excavated**, or dug out and explored, in 1907. By studying them, scientists figured out that the two men had died a few months apart. One was around 40 years old, and the other 60. The hieroglyphs in the tomb mentioned a woman named Khnum-Aa as the mother of both men, so the archaeologists named the mummies "The Two Brothers."

However, other archaeologists questioned whether the bodies were brothers. They said the shapes of their skulls and other bones were too different from each other to be related. Perhaps the hieroglyphs on the coffins were wrong? Perhaps the brothers were **adopted**?

Early attempts to test the DNA of both mummies did not work. However, in 2015, new tests on their teeth were successful. They showed that the two men did have the same mother—but they had different fathers. They were half-brothers.

11

GIZA—THE GREAT MYSTERY

The largest pyramid in Egypt is the Great Pyramid of Giza, which was built for Pharaoh Khufu. The pyramid holds many mysteries, including secret chambers and tunnels filled with traps to prevent thieves from robbing the pyramid. Scientists hope to send robots into some of the hidden areas to unlock more of their secrets.

Looking Through Stone

To see inside pyramids, forensic scientists use **cosmic rays** called muons. Cosmic rays hit Earth from outer space all the time. Muon rays are so small and fast that most of them pass straight through rock! Muon detectors are already used to help people search inside shipping containers to find **smuggled** (illegally transported) goods. Muons create a 3-D image similar to X-rays, but muons can pass through much thicker substances than most rays.

DID You Know?

Forensic analysis of the workers' skeletons buried near Giza show they were well cared for. Their bones show they had a healthy diet. However, the bones also showed signs of wear, breaks, and **arthritis**, proving that building pyramids was hard work!

This carving shows captured slaves. It was once thought that slaves such as these built the pyramids, but we now know that is not true (see opposite).

A Surprise Discovery

In 2015, archaeologists set up muon detectors around the Great Pyramid to help them see inside. They wanted to use the muon rays to map the inside of the pyramid without damaging it or anything that might be inside it. To their surprise, the archaeologists found a large hole in the middle of the pyramid. It is at least 98 feet (30 m) long. No one has yet been inside this hole, but some archaeologists are working on tiny robots that may be able to get inside the pyramid through tiny holes and look around.

*The pyramids at Giza were built so that no one could disturb the pharaoh buried inside, or all the objects and treasures he needed for the **afterlife**. By using scanners and detectors, experts can examine the inside of pyramids without ever needing to enter them.*

HOW SCIENCE SOLVED THE PAST:

MYSTERY OF THE PYRAMID BUILDERS

In the past, many people thought the pyramids were built by slaves. This was because historians from ancient Greece wrote that they believed 100,000 slaves were needed to build the pyramids. But were these workers actually slaves? Forensic scientists have uncovered the truth.

Near the pyramid, scientists discovered skeletons buried in shafts, with beer and bread for the afterlife. Scientists believe the skeletons belong to the people who built the pyramid. Tests on the bones show that the workers ate meat. This proved that the pyramid builders were not slaves but laborers who were fed well and buried with respect.

SECRETS OF THE MUMMIES

HOW SCIENCE SOLVED THE PAST:

HOW DID KING TUT DIE?

King Tutankhamun, also known as "King Tut," is perhaps the most famous ancient Egyptian pharaoh of all time. His tomb was discovered in 1922, and scientists have been trying to find out more about him ever since. We know from ancient writings that Tutankhamun died when he was 18, but how did he die? In 2010, forensic scientists looked at his body to learn more. They used the same techniques that forensic scientists use to examine bodies from modern crime scenes to figure out the cause and time of death.

Using CT scans and testing tissue samples, scientists found tiny living things called **parasites** in King Tut's body. His bones were also weak and badly formed. Based on this analysis, the scientists argued that Tutankhamun died of a combination of **malaria** (a disease caused by parasites in the blood, passed on by mosquitoes), and a bone disease.

Thanks to forensic tools such as **laser** scanners and **CT scans**, scientists can now uncover the secrets of the mummies without removing a single piece of cloth. Lasers use a beam of light to provide an accurate scan of the surface of an object. CT scans use X-rays to show what is under the surface of an object. Forensic scientists also use these technologies to scan crime scenes for clues and to test bodies to see how people might have died.

> Examining King Tut's body inside his beautiful coffin, scientists found that he suffered from weak bones.

From an ancient skull, scientists can use digital 3-D modeling to create a model of the dead person's face. This helps us see what that person might have looked like when he or she was alive.

DID
You Know?

Although many historians believe King Tut was weak and sickly, new forensic evidence claims he may have been a boy soldier. The remains of a leather tunic, used as armor, was found in his tomb. New forensic imaging techniques have revealed that the tunic had been worn often. Scientists say this shows that King Tut may even have gone into battle at some time in his life.

Scientists scan the cloth the mummy is wrapped in, then examine the hair and skin of the body. They look for substances that might have been used by the dead person such as cosmetics or medicine.

A Window to the Past

Scientists used CT and X-ray techniques to examine the mummy of a five-year-old ancient Egyptian girl who died more than 2,000 years ago. Using CT scanners, they looked through the coffin the girl was buried in and through the cloth she was wrapped in to see her bones and flesh. They could see the earrings, necklace, and **amulet** she was wearing. The CT scanner showed that the mummy still had black, curly hair.

MYSTERIOUS MUMMIES

Dying of old age was uncommon for most ancient peoples, including the Egyptians. They did not have the medicines we use today, so even minor diseases and injuries could result in death. In fact, most ancient Egyptians died before they were 30 years old! With death always lurking, it is not surprising the ancient Egyptians spent a lot of time thinking about death—and what to do with their bodies once they had died.

Historical Clues and Forensic Footprints

Egyptians believed they would need a physical body after death to move on to the afterlife. The body of the dead person was preserved using a process called mummification. For centuries, historians were unable to unlock the mysteries of Egyptian mummies. Who had these people been in life, and how had they died? Historians did not have the tools to answer these questions—until now.

Forensic scientists can test bones, skin, and hair from mummies. What they cannot always test are the organs of a body, which were removed before mummification.

Science Shines a Light

The arrival of modern forensic science meant that mummification could be accurately investigated for the first time. Now, scientists could examine mummies in detail—**analyzing** the materials they were wrapped in, the contents of their bodies, and how they had been preserved. The age of mummies could also be figured out, using a technique called **carbon dating**. All living things contain a type of **carbon** that decays at a fixed rate, even after death. So, measuring the amount of carbon in something is a way to figure out its age.

HOW SCIENCE SOLVED THE PAST:

THE LONG-LOST QUEEN HATSHEPSUT

A single tooth brought an end to the long search for Queen Hatshepsut, the most famous queen to rule ancient Egypt. For hundreds of years, historians had searched for her body, without success. CT scans matched an unidentified mummy to a tooth from a jar marked with her name. Further testing matched the mummy's DNA to Hatshepsut's family. The tests revealed she had died of cancer at about age 50. The DNA evidence helped scientists figure out that the 3,500-year-old mummy it came from really was that of Hatshepsut!

DID You Know?

The ancient Egyptians even mummified their pet cats! Mummies of cats, such as the one shown at left, have been found throughout Egypt. Carbon dating helps scientists discover how old a mummy is and in which ancient Egyptian **era** it was made.

 Forensic tests showed that cats were mummified in the same way as humans.

THE POWER OF BLUE POWDER

A blue powder made by the ancient Egyptians thousands of years ago could help solve crimes today. The blue powder was mixed with a liquid to make paint. When archaeologists were examining tombs, they noticed that some areas of painted walls or coffins glowed when they shone a red light on them.

Glowing Color

Forensic scientists discovered that the color blue used by the ancient Egyptians gives out **infrared** rays when a red light is shone onto it, making it glow. They discovered that they could detect small glowing traces of this blue color with red light, even if the traces were too small for the eye to see. The forensic scientists called the color Egyptian Blue. They are now developing a technique that can help police solve crimes, using the same Egyptian Blue that was used in ancient Egypt thousands of years ago!

Egyptian Blue, used to color this painting thousands of years ago, is today being used to catch criminals.

A Forensic Breakthrough

At a crime scene, forensic scientists dust surfaces for fingerprints. They use a small brush to cover a surface with powder. The powder sticks to the oil left by fingerprints and forms the pattern of the fingerprints that the police can then use to identify criminals. However, these fingerprints can be hard to see, especially on shiny or patterned surfaces. Forensic scientists think they can solve this by using Egyptian Blue.

Scientists have tested different surfaces with Egyptian Blue powder. They shine a red light on the blue powder and take a photograph using a digital camera with special infrared light filters. The camera captures the glowing fingerprints that can be used as evidence by the police.

*We have long thought that all ancient Egyptians had dark hair, as shown on this statue of a **scribe**. However, thanks to forensic analysis (see below) we now know some ancient Egyptians were fair-haired.*

HOW SCIENCE SOLVED THE PAST:

A COLORFUL PAST

Today, many ancient Egyptian statues and **artifacts** look a dull brown or gray. Any colorful paint they once had has been destroyed over time. Scientists can recreate how these objects might have looked by searching for the glowing Egyptian Blue paint, using infrared light. Using this and other forensic tests, plus computer modeling, scientists can recreate the objects as they might have looked when they were first made, thousands of years ago.

DID You Know?

Many historians believed that ancient Egyptians had black or brown hair. Although fair-haired mummies have been found, experts thought their hair had changed from dark to light because of the mummification process. Following chemical experiments on 16 samples of hair from mummies of all ages, scientists now believe some ancient Egyptians were natural blonds.

IN SEARCH OF A QUEEN

Queen Nefertiti was the wife of the pharaoh Akhenaten, who was the father of Tutankhamun. The **bust** of Nefertiti's head is one of the most recognized ancient Egyptian artifacts in the world, but her life remains a mystery. There are no records about when and how Nefertiti died, and her mummy has never been found.

Whose Tomb?

Searchers for Nefertiti started to look at King Tut's tomb. Historians noted that King Tut's tomb was smaller than other pharaoh tombs. Artifacts appeared to be hastily placed inside, suggesting Tutankhamun had died suddenly. Perhaps he had been buried in a queen's tomb because a grander tomb was not ready? Could the tomb, in fact, be Nefertiti's tomb?

> This is the famous bust of Queen Nefertiti. If her body is ever found, **genetic** scientists will be able to study DNA samples from it to see if Nefertiti is the mother of King Tut (see opposite).

Secret Doors

Scientists used laser scanners to create a 3-D model of King Tut's tomb. This showed that there might be two doors in one wall that could have been plastered and painted over. However, in 2018, forensic experts scanned the tomb using **ground penetrating radar (GPR)** and found no evidence of hidden chambers. So, the search for Nefertiti goes on!

This carving shows Queen Nefertiti and King Akhenaten with two children. Could one of them have been King Tut?

DID You Know?

Nefertiti's bust suggests that her eyes had an unusual feature–the inner part of the eye drops down toward her nose. She may have had an eye defect that was passed down genetically through her family. If Nefertiti's mummy is found, scientists could discover the DNA code that created her eyes. They could then use that information to analyze other mummies to see if the DNA code matches. This would show if they are Nefertiti's children.

PAPER TRAIL

The ancient Egyptians were one of the first civilizations to use writing material similar to paper. They made this material from the leaves of the papyrus plant. In fact, the word paper comes from "papyrus."

Invisible Ink

One of the challenges of analyzing papyrus is that the ink used to write on it fades over time. However, forensic scientists have already developed techniques to look for faded ink on old or damaged documents. X-ray scanners can detect traces of ink invisible to the eye. They can also spot dents in the paper where the writing once was.

HOW SCIENCE SOLVED THE PAST:

THE BOOK OF THE DEAD

The Book of the Dead contained spells that could be used in the afterlife. It is not a book with pages. It is a **scroll** made from papyrus. Rich families ordered copies of it to be buried with the dead. One copy was found in the tomb of Ramose, a man who died in around 1250 B.C E. It was in thousands of pieces. Experts at the Fitzwilliam Museum in Cambridge, England, pieced together the scroll like a jigsaw puzzle. But they needed to know exactly what the scroll and ink were made from. Forensic scientists tested samples of the papyrus and found colors based on materials such as the metal copper and a poisonous substance called arsenic sulfide.

Scribes, seen in this carving, played an important role in ancient Egypt. They copied books such as the Book of the Dead. Scientists can now scan their faded writings, so we can read them and learn more about ancient Egypt.

Paper Pile

In 2013, 30 mysterious rolls of papyrus were found in caves near the Dead Sea in Egypt. Scientists used forensic testing techniques, such as carbon dating, to discover that they are more than 4,500 years old. This makes them the oldest papyrus documents ever found! They were written during the time of King Khufu, whose pyramid is the Great Pyramid of Giza.

Wrapped in Spells

Scrolls of the Book of the Dead could be up to 65 feet (20 m) long. They contain "spells" that helped the dead travel safely to the afterlife. Scientists examining mummies have found bodies wrapped in spells from the Book of the Dead, written on the linen strips. Unwrapping the strips could destroy them because they are so old, so the scientists use forensic scanning techniques to examine the cloth without damaging it.

⌃ *This scene from the Book of the Dead is written on papyrus. Scientists have dated it to around 1275 B.C.E. It shows a dead person's heart being weighed against a feather. If the heart is the same weight as the feather, the person can enter the afterlife. If the heart is heavier, then he will spend forever in the underworld.*

DID You Know?

Infrared photography has revealed that the name of the owner of one Book of the Dead was painted out. Historians believe it may be because the owner could not pay for the book, so it was probably given to someone who could afford it!

BRINGING MUMMIES BACK TO LIFE!

What did the ancient Egyptians actually look like? Art and science have combined to help us find out. Scientists can use CT scanning and 3-D printing to **reconstruct** bodies that have rotted away. **Genetic scans** of bones and skin samples can pinpoint the age of bodies. They can also reveal if they were male or female.

Meet Meritamun

Scientists at the University of Melbourne, in Australia, decided to study the skull of an Egyptian woman who died between 2,000 and 3,500 years ago. Forensic scientists carried out a CT scan of her skull, and a computer image was made from the scan. Experts then altered the shape of the skull to make it look as it would have before the body was mummified. Finally, scientists used a 3-D printer to print a 3-D plastic model of the skull.

« Forensic scientists examine skulls for clues to a dead person's age and whether the person is male or female. Then, they can begin facial reconstruction. Scientists wear gloves to make sure their DNA does not mix with any DNA from the skull.

DID
You Know?

Archaeologists are working to get to know Meritamun even better. Carbon dating of her skull will help reveal when she died. Studies of Meritamun's skull will also tell historians more about her health and diet.

Experts looked carefully at the size and shape of the jaw. They saw the skull had rounded eye sockets, and that the top part of the mouth was narrow. From this, they could tell that the skull belonged to a female. They named her Meritamun. By measuring her bones, experts can tell us that she was just over 5 feet (1.5 m) tall.

HOW SCIENCE SOLVED THE PAST:

RETURN OF THE MUMMY!

To bring Meritamun to life, a forensic sculptor began with the model of the skull. She used markers (pins) to show where the skull's tissues and muscles would have been, based on information scientists already have on how ancient Egyptians looked. Using the markers, the sculptor modeled her face from **clay**. This created a realistic model of Meritamun, showing us how she might have looked when she was alive.

The sculptor had to guess at things such as hair color and style, as well as skin tone. She did have clues, though. There were drawings the Egyptians made of themselves, their hairstyles, and clothing. Finally, the lifelike figure of Meritamun was revealed. She looked very good for someone more than 2,000 years old!

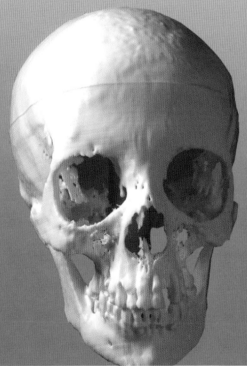

A 3-D printout of a skull was used as the base for building the face of Meritamun (shown right).

PLANT-ED CLUES!

There is more to ancient Egypt than pyramids, mummies, and tombs. Archaeologists can learn a lot from the plants they find from ancient times. However, it is only in the past 50 years that scientists have tried to find out what plants can tell us about the world in which the ancient Egyptians lived.

Plant Detectives

Forensic botanists study plant remains found at crime scenes. The study of **pollen** and seeds can help them identify where a crime has taken place, how a person died, and if a body has been moved.

Plant clues are often not at all obvious. Forensic scientists have to carry out chemical tests on soil, jar scrapings, and other remains to find the pollen, seeds, and other tiny fragments that can help identify plants and trees.

HISTORY'S HEALERS

Forensic chemists have studied the **residue** inside pottery jars used by the ancient Egyptians. In the residue, they found traces of grape wine, but also herbs and tree **resins** that were added to the wine. Could these have been used as medicines? Ancient Egyptian medical texts show more than 1,000 pictures of medicines, and all have names. But only 20 percent of the names have been **translated**. New forensic testing of residue is telling us more about the fruits, vegetables, herbs, and oils the ancient Egyptians used in their medicines.

Studying the plants found at ancient Egyptian archaeological sites tells us about the **climate** the Egyptians lived in. It tells us what they ate, and what perfumes, cosmetics, and dyes they used. Thanks to forensic science, we know that the ancient Egyptians used large amounts of tree resins called frankincense and myrrh. The trees did not grow locally in Egypt, which means the Egyptians must have traveled to faraway places to find them.

Not all jars contained food or drink. The canopic jars shown below contained a dead person's organs, such as the liver and stomach. The ancient Egyptians believed that people would need their organs in the afterlife. During mummification, the organs were removed and stored in jars. The jars were then buried with the mummy.

DID You Know?

Lord Carnarvon, the man who paid for the discovery of King Tutankhamun's tomb, died soon after. Some blamed his death on the "Curse of the Pharaohs," which was believed to kill people who disturbed the dead. Had he been cursed? Tests on Tutankhamun's tomb found two dangerous types of **mold**. Both cause **pneumonia** if breathed in. However, Carnarvon actually died after being bitten by a mosquito, then getting an infection. He may not have been "cursed," but scientists now wear protective clothing and masks to keep safe while working on mummies.

FORENSIC FUTURE

In spite of all we have learned about the ancient Egyptians, we may never discover all the details of their lives. However, with the help of forensic science, even the smallest clues have given archaeologists and historians a clearer picture of what life was like in ancient Egypt. DNA analysis has revealed how Egyptians were related and how they died. Chemical tests have shown us what the Egyptians ate and what medicines they made. Using muon detectors, we have found hidden spaces inside pyramids.

Forensic science is improving all the time. Soon, better MRI and CT scans will allow us to examine mummies in greater detail without damaging them. Computers are helping us build even better 3-D models of buildings and people. Infrared technology is revealing writing that was once hidden to the world. Who knows what mysteries we will solve in the future thanks to forensic science!

>> Tests can show if a piece of ancient stone has any paint that cannot be seen by the human eye.

DID You Know?

Traces of colored paint have been found on the Great Sphinx (see right). Scientists believe the Sphinx may have had a painted red face and its body may have been painted in bright colors such as blue and yellow. Infrared and chemical testing may help prove how bright the Sphinx really was.

CAN FORENSICS SOLVE...?

Here are two of the biggest unsolved mysteries about ancient Egypt. Forensic scientists are using forensic footprints to try to solve these mysteries, too!

The Secret of the Sphinx

One of the biggest mysteries still to be solved is the Sphinx at Giza. The Sphinx is higher than a six-story building. It was carved out of solid rock, although no one knows exactly when. Some archaeologists wonder if there is anything underneath the Sphinx, such as tunnels leading from other sites at Giza. Maybe with the development of CT and muon scanning, secret passageways beneath the Sphinx could one day be revealed.

The Screaming Mummy

In 1886, a partly mummified body was discovered that looked as though it was screaming in pain. No one knows exactly why, but the most popular theories are that the person was poisoned, buried alive, or hanged and died in agony. But who is the mummy—and was he murdered? One investigation said it could be Prince Pentewere, son of Pharaoh Ramses III, who was suspected of planning his father's murder. Maybe his plan was discovered and he was poisoned as a punishment. His scream could be from the pain of the poison. Others believe the "scream" is due to his head being pushed back after death and his jaw forced open, so it is not a scream at all. Future forensic tests could find out if his bones contain poison or not, and DNA tests may reveal the true identity of the mysterious screaming mummy.

> ≫ Carbon dating does not work on stone, so forensic scientists will have to find other ways to figure out the exact age of the Great Sphinx.

GLOSSARY

Please note: Some **bold-faced** words are defined where they appear in the book.

abscesses Infections, often beneath teeth

adopted To bring a child into your family and raise the child as your own

afterlife A life after death

amulet A type of jewelry worn on a string around the neck, usually to protect a person from bad luck or to bring them good luck

analyzing Studying something carefully

anthropologists Experts who study who ancient people were, how they lived, and where they came from

archaeologists Experts who study where ancient people lived and the things they left behind

arteries Major blood vessels leading from the heart

artifacts Old objects usually made by someone

arthritis A disease of the joints that causes swelling and can be very painful

bust A sculpture showing only a person's head, shoulders, and upper chest

calcium A hard substance found in bones and teeth

carbon A chemical found in all living plants and animals

cavities Holes that have been worn away inside something, often a tooth

cells The smallest working pieces of a living thing that are part of all living things

civilizations Settled and stable communities in which people live together peacefully and use systems such as writing to communicate

clay A heavy, sticky material that can be shaped easily and becomes hard when baked

climate The type of weather a place has over a long period of time

cosmic rays Forms of energy that come from the Sun

decayed Rotted

DNA Material that contains all of the information needed to create an individual living thing

era An important period in history

evidence Facts and information that tell us whether something is true

forensic botanists Scientists who examine plants to try to solve crimes

forensic science The use of scientific methods and techniques to find clues about crimes or the past

foundations Solid structures that support a building from underneath

genetic To do with genes, which are the parts of cells that make up all living things and hold all the information needed to make us who we are, such as hair and skin color

genetic scans Tests on a person's genes to find links to other family members, or to find any signs of illnesses that might happen to that person

ground penetrating radar (GPR) A machine that draws a map of what is underground by sending energy pulses into the earth that bounce back when they hit buildings or other objects

hieroglyphs Pictures representing a word, syllable, or sound

identity Who or what someone or something is

infrared A type of light that feels warm but cannot be seen

magnetic resonance imaging (MRI) A machine that uses strong magnets and radio waves to look inside objects and create a picture of what is inside

microscopes Devices used to see objects that are too small to be seen by the naked eye

mold A fuzzy substance that grows on damp or decaying material

molecule The smallest part of something that looks and behaves in the same way as the thing that it is a part of

mummified Describing a body that has been preserved by wrapping it in special cloths or linens and drying out the flesh

parasites Organisms that live inside the body of another living thing, feeding off of it and making it sick